# Is socialist revolution in the U.S. possible?

# Is socialist revolution in the U.S. possible?

## A NECESSARY DEBATE

## Mary-Alice Waters

## PATHFINDER

NEW YORK    LONDON    MONTREAL    SYDNEY

ISBN 978-1-60488-018-2
Library of Congress Control Number: 2008943740
Manufactured in the United States of America

First edition, 2008
Second edition, 2009

COVER DESIGN: Eric Simpson

COVER PHOTO: April 10, 2006: 500,000 people march in Washington, D.C., to demand legalization of undocumented immigrants. More than a million joined demonstrations that day across the U.S. On May Day, three weeks later, more than two million workers stayed off the job and poured into the streets in over 140 cities and towns in the United States, as that historic working-class holiday began fighting to be reborn as a *day of struggle*. (Associated Press)

**Pathfinder**
www.pathfinderpress.com
E-mail: pathfinder@pathfinderpress.com

# CONTENTS

# PREFACE TO SECOND EDITION

This expanded 2009 edition of *Is Socialist Revolution in the U.S. Possible?* is being released in the midst of an accelerating worldwide contraction of capitalist production and jobs of historic magnitude. The unfolding economic, financial, and social crisis will, over time, spur increasing resistance by working people to defend our class and its allies and to strengthen the unions. The deepening disorder of world capitalism—and the working-class battles, proletarian solidarity, and more and more disciplined organization that will grow—increase the stakes for humanity in how the question posed in the title of this book is, in practice, resolved.

Like the first edition, published in 2008, the book is built around the talk given by Mary-Alice Waters, president of Pathfinder Press, that opened a five-day rolling panel discussion on "The United States: a possible revolution"—the central forum planned and hosted by organizers of the 2007 Venezuela International Book Fair held in Caracas. That presentation appears along with an account from the pages of the *Militant* newspaper on the week-long political exchange involving twenty-two panelists and several hundred audience participants.

A year later the Venezuelan publishing house Monte Ávila published an edition of *Is Socialist Revolution in the U.S. Possible?* for sale in bookstores throughout that country and distributed a thousand copies of a special

7

printing free to participants during the November 2008 international book fair. Speaking at the Caracas launching of the title on November 14 were Carolina Álvarez, Monte Ávila's editorial director; Erick Rangel, a national leader of the youth of the governing United Socialist Party of Venezuela and student at Central University of Venezuela in Caracas; José González, president of the ALBA Cultural Fund; and Waters.

This new edition includes the talk by Mary-Alice Waters at that event.

*Norton Sandler*
*January 2009*

# INTRODUCTION

*by Norton Sandler*

The central political event of the 2007 Venezuela International Book Fair held in Caracas was a five-day rolling forum on "The United States: a possible revolution."

The timely initiative by Venezuela's National Book Center in organizing this forum "opens discussion on a question the answer to which, in practice, will ultimately determine the future of humanity—or more accurately perhaps, whether there *is* a future for humanity," said Mary-Alice Waters in her remarks kicking off what became a wide-ranging debate at the event.

This pamphlet contains Waters's opening presentation, as well as coverage of the lively five-day exchange from the pages of the U.S. socialist newsweekly, the *Militant*. Waters, a member of the Socialist Workers Party National Committee and president of Pathfinder Press, edited and wrote the preface to Pathfinder's *Cuba and the Coming American Revolution* by Jack Barnes, which she drew on in her remarks. The book—among the titles recently issued in Venezuela by Monte Ávila, one of that country's leading publishers—was presented at the fair at meetings sponsored both by Monte Ávila and by Pathfinder.

Some twenty-two participants addressed the November 10–14 forum, almost all of whom had long been involved in various social protest movements and political parties in the United States. Several currently live in Venezuela, but the majority traveled from North America to take part.

Widely diverging and often sharply counterposed views were debated in the course of what was, with one exception, a model of civil debate for the workers movement. The exchange achieved an unusual degree of clarity on a number of central political questions. The resolution of those questions, in the course of far-reaching class struggle, will decide whether the working class in the United States will be able to transform itself into a class with a mass political vanguard capable of successfully leading broad layers of oppressed and exploited toilers in a struggle for power.

Most sessions of the central forum were attended by 125–150 participants. The importance of the issues addressed in the Caracas debate, which were reported in newspapers and on radio and television in Venezuela, is what prompted Pathfinder to produce this pamphlet. The two-part article reprinted here by Olympia Newton, who covered the forum for the *Militant*, describes the rich debate as it unfolded around five central questions.

### 1. The weight and importance of a historic new wave of immigration to the United States

Over the last two decades, millions of workers from across the Americas and the world have been brought into the mines, factories, fields, and service industries in the United States. This has resulted in strengthening the resistance and combativity of toilers in face of the bosses' quarter-century-plus drive to brutally intensify production line speeds, lengthen the workday, and slash wages, health and retirement benefits, and workers compensation.

This immigration, which is transforming the vanguard of the U.S. working class, is "the most important political development in the United States," said Waters, who had been asked by forum organizers to lead off the panel the opening day. She pointed out that millions of workers had poured into the streets across the country on May Day in 2006 and 2007, taking the U.S. rulers by surprise. That "historic working-class holiday is fighting to be reborn in the United States as a day of *struggle*," she said.

"A fighting vanguard of the working class has emerged in action" in the United States and "is already placing its mark on politics and the class struggle." It is a working-class vanguard, not just a vanguard of immigrants, Waters said. And it is the biggest long-term political problem the U.S. rulers face, because the labor of workers, native- and foreign-born, is the major source of the propertied families' wealth and power. They have come to "utterly depend on this massive pool of superexploited labor. They cannot compete worldwide and accumulate capital without it."

That's why "the battle to win the vast majority of the working class and the entire labor movement to support the legalization of undocumented immigrants is the single most important 'domestic' political question in the United States," Waters said, "and the largest current battle on the road to independent working-class political action, to a labor party based on a militant, fighting union movement."

This perspective, and a course of action for the working-class vanguard consistent with it, was sharply rejected by several panelists as well as by others in the audience. Speaking immediately after Waters, Venezuelan-American lawyer and author Eva Golinger spelled out a counterposed view. Far from taking a vanguard place in growing resistance to the employers' accelerated exploitation, Golinger said, immigrant workers in the United States simply want to live in "a capitalist consumer society" and get a piece of the pie for themselves. They believe what Fox News and CNN tell them, she added. "People are not poor or hungry in the United States like they were in Venezuela," she argued. "You get two or three credit cards in the mail every day. There is poverty but only in a few small sectors." Golinger said she didn't share Waters's "optimism that a revolution is possible in the United States."

A number of other speakers over the five days expressed similar contempt for the tens of millions of toilers of the Americas, Africa, and Asia, forced by economic realities of imperialist domination in their homelands to find their way to the United States or other economically advanced capitalist countries. To do so, these workers often risk their lives to get into the United States to seek jobs, to survive under intense exploitation, and to send a few dollars home to their families.

As Newton describes in these pages, numerous other panelists, including several who had themselves emigrated to the United States, countered such views just as vigorously.

### 2. The battle to unite the working class against the divide-and-rule strategies of the capitalist class, upon which their domination rests

As Waters noted, a sharpening capitalist financial and economic crisis like that opening today "will intensify the battle for the political soul of the working class" in face of efforts by the employers to turn immigrants, workers who are Black or female, and others into scapegoats for mounting joblessness and worsening economic and social conditions.

Working people in the United States "face the same class enemy," Waters said, "and determined struggles on any front tend to pull workers together in face of the attempts to divide us." More than ever before in history, she emphasized, a fighting vanguard capable of leading a successful revolutionary struggle in the United States today will bring together workers regardless of skin color, national origin, or sex. As we fight alongside each other, "it becomes harder for the bosses to pit 'us' against 'them,'" she pointed out. "It becomes more possible to see that our class interests are not the same as those of 'our' bosses, 'our' government, or 'our' two parties."

A counterview to this perspective was expressed most sharply by panelist Amiri Baraka, a U.S. writer who has been active in Black nationalist, Maoist, and Democratic Party politics since the 1960s. Baraka argued strongly that "white privilege" has derailed all potentially revolutionary struggles in U.S. history, including the powerful labor upsurge of the 1930s and the mass movement that brought down the institution of Jim Crow segregation in the South by the end of the 1960s. The failure of the "white left" to organize "whites" to fight "white privilege," he said, has spelled the doom of every movement for social change.

In this version of history, race-baiting rears its ugly head, as "white workers" with racist prejudices become the explanation for all defeats. Missing is the responsibility borne by Stalinist parties, from the mid-1930s on, for subordinating struggles by working people and the oppressed worldwide to Moscow's quest for peaceful coexistence with the imperialist rulers. In the United States that meant diverting the great social movement that grew out of the battle to organize the industrial unions, channelling it toward support for the Democratic Party. (In her remarks, Waters had pointed out that as a result of such Stalinist political misleadership, "The revolutionary potential of the great radicalization in the 1930s was squandered and diverted into support for capitalism's 'New Deal' and its inevitable accompaniment, the 'War Deal'—the imperialist slaughter of World War II." With the collapse of Stalinist regimes in the Soviet Union and Eastern Europe in the late 1980s and early 1990s, she said, that "enormous political obstacle no longer stands across the road toward independent working-class political action and revolutionary socialist leadership.")

Participants in the audience pointed to examples of strikes and other recent struggles in the United States in which the employers have failed to achieve their objectives with divide-and-rule strategies that had long proved effective.

In response, Baraka said he did not share the opinion expressed by others that racial divisions could be overcome through such struggles, because "white leaders" are interested above all in protecting their privileged positions. In short, "white privilege" is more powerful than common class interests.

### 3. The poison of Jew-hatred and agent-baiting in the working-class movement and movements for national liberation

Other sharp assaults against the integrity of the workers movement were confronted during the forum as well. The toxins of Jew-hatred and agent-baiting were introduced. As always, they were intertwined with attempts to explain history as the work of powerful, unknown forces conspiring against the oppressed and exploited—rather than the scientific view advanced by Marx and Engels that "the history of all hitherto existing society is the history of class struggles." That view, presented in the Communist Manifesto, has been the foundation of the modern workers movement ever since.

Early in the forum, a speaker who said he was visiting from Panama declared from the floor that Jews "have all the money" and control everything from the international banking system and powerful imperialist media conglomerates to U.S. foreign policy, especially policy toward the Middle East. This myth, infecting growing layers of middle-class liberals and radicals in the United States and other imperialist countries today, is also widely advanced throughout Latin America, including among those who are otherwise staunch anti-imperialists.

On the closing day of the forum, Baraka ended his presentation by reading his verse about the events of September 11, 2001, entitled "Somebody Blew Up America." That piece asks: "Who knew the World Trade Center was gonna get bombed / Who told 4000 Israeli workers at the Twin Towers / To stay home that day / Why did Sharon stay away?"

These bigoted, conspiracy-spinning allegations deny not only the facts of what happened on September 11, they conceal the plain truth of how capitalism works. Above all, they deprive working people of the knowledge and confidence that we are the makers of history—that our own conscious, revolutionary action, and only that, can remove the capitalist ruling families from power and prevent them from blowing up the world.

Following the initial remarks in the discusson period about the rich and all-powerful Jews, I took the floor to point out that Jew-hatred remains one of the most virulent anti-working-class weapons of the ruling classes, as it has been for the past century and a half. Recalling its ghastly consequences in the hands of Germany's imperialist rulers in the 1930s and '40s, I underlined the deadly threat to the workers movement of refusing to intransigently combat any and all scapegoating of Jews, Latinos, Blacks, gypsies, whites, or any other national or ethnic grouping.

Agent-baiting was also introduced into the debate—the one departure from civil discussion noted earlier—and it was answered. Baraka accused one fellow panelist of hiding that he was a "Trotskyite" and another of being an "agent" (of some unnamed power) whose objective was to abet the mobilization of a reactionary student movement in the streets of Venezuela to overthrow the elected government of Hugo Chávez.

Waters replied to Baraka. Thanking book fair organizers for making possible the expression of a broad range of views as part of the forum, she stressed that in order for civil debate to take place, "the poison of agent- and race-baiting" must be condemned by all.

### 4. The history and legacy of revolutionary struggle in the United States

"There has never been a revolution in the United States, and anyone who thinks there has been is ignorant of their own history," argued British journalist Richard Gott. He contended that even the first bourgeois-democratic revolution in North America at the end of the 1700s—which broke the imperial domination of the thirteen colonies by the British monarchy and the English landed and merchant classes—had not been a revolution but simply a reactionary land-grab by the U.S. colonial bourgeoisie.

Other forum participants, especially a number from Venezuela and elsewhere in Latin America, concurred with that view. Some added that the second American revolution, the 1861–65 U.S. Civil War that abolished chattel slavery, had not been a revolution either, since the Union Army had not from the beginning mobilized freed slaves into its ranks.

Panelist Lee Sustar, the labor editor of *Socialist Worker*, a publication of the International Socialist Organization in the United States, put forward a different view. "The United States was created by revolution," Sustar explained. The Civil War, he stated, was the completion of the bourgeois-democratic revolution begun with the war for independence from the British crown.

Amiri Baraka agreed that the United States has already known two revolutions, but he argued sharply that the bourgeois-democratic goal of those revolutions has not yet been achieved. "The property question was settled. Chattel slavery was eliminated," Baraka said. "But the democratic revolution has never been completed." As evidence of the assertion, Baraka pointed out that Blacks aren't equal and there is no democracy in the United States. The fact that no bourgeois-democratic revolution anywhere in the world has ever brought—or ever sought to achieve—equality and democracy for the oppressed and exploited majority was conveniently ignored.

### 5. Revolutionary prospects for workers and farmers in the United States today and tomorrow

Such disputed questions of history were not arcane differences of no consequence for today. Those arguing most strongly that no revolution has ever taken place in the United States were among the most vociferous in insisting that working people in the U.S. are incapable of revolutionary struggle now or in the future. "The only hope is Latin America," concluded Richard Gott. Eva Golinger argued that "the only way to achieve structural change in the United States is to make advances here" in Venezuela.

For Amiri Baraka the conclusion was obvious too. If the bourgeois-democratic revolution was incomplete, then bourgeois reform is what's on the agenda in the United States today. He laid out his program to complete that task as part of a bloc with sections of the Black bourgeoisie. The program he spelled out was aimed not at advancing a revolutionary struggle by the working class and its allies to take power out of the hands of the capitalist rulers. Instead,

Baraka advocated rewriting the bourgeois constitution of the United States and replacing the current bicameral Congress with a unicameral parliamentary system similar to what exists in the big majority of imperialist powers!

Nothing could have been in sharper contrast to Waters's opening remarks that, "Yes, revolution *is* possible in the United States. Socialist revolution. To put it in class terms, a proletarian revolution—the broadest, most inclusive social upheaval of the oppressed and exploited imaginable, and the reorganization of society in their interests. . . .

"What's more, revolutionary *struggle* by the toilers along the path I just described is *inevitable*." What is not inevitable, however, Waters emphasized, "is the outcome of these coming revolutionary struggles. . . . That is why what we do *now*, while there is time to prepare—what kind of nucleus of what kind of revolutionary organization we build today—weighs so heavily."

These were the important issues discussed and debated in the Caracas forum on "The United States: a possible revolution." And the reason why this record of that debate will be of substantial interest, far beyond those who participated in it.

*March 2008*

# ABOUT THE AUTHORS

**Mary-Alice Waters** is a member of the Socialist Workers Party National Committee. She is editor of *New International* and president of Pathfinder Press. Waters is editor of Pathfinder's nineteen-book series on the Cuban Revolution in world politics and has edited and contributed to numerous other Pathfinder books and pamphlets, including *Rosa Luxemburg Speaks*, *The Changing Face of U.S. Politics*, *Capitalism's World Disorder*, and *Cosmetics, Fashions, and the Exploitation of Women*.

**Olympia Newton** covered the 2007 Venezuela International Book Fair for the *Militant*, a socialist newsweekly published in New York.

**Norton Sandler** is a member of the Socialist Workers Party National Committee and a longtime leader of the party's trade union work. He organizes the efforts to expand circulation of Pathfinder books and pamphlets throughout the Americas.

PHOTOS: MAGGIE TROWE/MILITANT

*"The theme for this event, 'The United States: a possible revolution,' opens discussion on a question the answer to which will ultimately determine the future of humanity."*

**Top:** Opening day of November 2007 forum. Speaking, Mary-Alice Waters, president of Pathfinder Press. Others, left to right, are lawyer and author Eva Golinger and moderator Luis Bilbao, an Argentine journalist.
**Bottom:** Closing day of forum. Speaking, writer Amiri Baraka. Others, left to right, are meditation teacher Dada Maheshvarananda; researcher Steve Brouwer; moderator Iván Padilla, Venezuela's deputy minister of culture for human development; and poet Amina Baraka.

# Is socialist revolution in the U.S. possible?

## by Mary-Alice Waters

First of all, I want to thank CENAL (the National Book Center) and the organizers of the 2007 Venezuela Book Fair for their choice of the theme for this event. "The United States: a possible revolution" opens discussion on a question whose answer, in practice, will ultimately determine the future of humanity—or more accurately perhaps, whether there *is* a future for humanity.

I am speaking here today as one of a small minority, including among those who call themselves leftists, or revolutionaries, a minority that says without hesitation or qualification: Yes, revolution *is* possible in the United States. Socialist revolution. To put it in class terms, a proletarian revolution—the broadest, most inclusive social upheaval of the oppressed and exploited imaginable, and

*This was the opening presentation to the November 10–14 central forum of the 2007 Venezuela International Book Fair whose theme was "The United States: a possible revolution."*

the reorganization of society in their interests.

As it deepens, that mass revolutionary struggle will win the support of the *majority* of the working class, small farmers, and other exploited producers and their powerful allies among oppressed nationalities, women, and others. It will be led by an increasingly class-conscious, tested, and expanding political vanguard of the working class.

In the third American revolution, workers who are African-American will be a disproportionately large component of the leadership.

That revolutionary struggle will take political and military power from the class that today holds it, mobilizing the strength and solidarity—the humanity—of working people in the United States on the side of the oppressed and exploited worldwide.

It will be a struggle that transforms the men and women who carry it forward as they fight to transform the twisted social relations inherited from the dog-eat-dog world of capitalism—relations that corrode human solidarity and coarsen us all.

What's more, revolutionary *struggle* by the toilers along the path I just described is *inevitable*. It will be initiated at first not by the toilers, but forced upon us by the crisis-driven assaults of the propertied classes. And our struggles will be intertwined, as always, with the resistance and struggles of other oppressed and exploited producers around the globe.

What is *not* inevitable, however, is the outcome of these coming revolutionary struggles. That is where political clarity, organization, discipline, and the caliber of proletarian leadership become decisive. That is why what we do *now*, while there is still time to prepare—what kind of nucleus of what kind of revolutionary organization we build today—weighs so heavily.

I wanted to assert this at the start so our discussion here at this event can share a common vocabulary. This is the meaningful *class* content I give the oft-abused word "revolution."

## Cuba and Coming American Revolution

One of the books being presented at this festival by Monte Ávila, one of the leading publishers here in Venezuela, bears the title *Cuba and the Coming American Revolution*. It was written by Jack Barnes and first published by Pathfinder Press in 2001. I mention it at the outset not just to salute the editors of Monte Ávila for their political perspicacity, and perhaps audacity, in publishing this new, 2007 edition of the book. More importantly, I want to introduce the book's theme as a part of our discussion.

*Cuba and the Coming American Revolution* is not primarily about the Cuban Revolution that triumphed on January 1, 1959—although it *is* about the worldwide impact of that revolution. As the back cover notes, it is, above all, "about the struggles of working people in the imperialist heartland, the youth who are attracted to them, and the example set by the people of Cuba that revolution is not only necessary, it can be made.

"It is about the class struggle in the United States, where the revolutionary capacities of workers and farmers are today as utterly discounted by the ruling powers as were those of the Cuban toilers. And just as wrongly."

The book highlights a statement made by Cuban leader-Fidel Castro almost forty-seven years ago, on the eve of the U.S.-organized invasion of Cuba at the Bay of Pigs.[1]

---

1. On April 17, 1961, 1,500 Cuban-born mercenaries, organized and armed by Washington, invaded Cuba at the Bay of Pigs on the southern coast. The invaders were defeated in less than seventy-two hours by the

That abortive April 1961 assault was undoubtedly imperialism's greatest miscalculation in the history of our hemisphere, a blunder born of colossal class arrogance and class blindness on the part of those who considered themselves to be the rightful owners of all that the land and the toilers of Cuba together produced. That miscalculation ended at Playa Girón in the glory of the first military defeat of Washington in the Americas.

A month before, in March 1961, Fidel told a cheering crowd of Cuban workers, farmers, and youth, "There will be a victorious revolution in the United States before a victorious counterrevolution in Cuba."

At the time, many of us on both sides of the Florida Straits knew that statement was not empty bravado, nor was Fidel gazing in a crystal ball. He was speaking as a leader offering—*advancing*—a line of struggle for our lifetimes. He was addressing the question "What is to be done?"—both in Cuba and in the United States.

Each succeeding generation of revolutionaries has carried those words on our banner, with the determination to speed the day they will be fully realized.

Today, that flag is being held high by five Cuban revolutionaries now in their tenth year of imprisonment in the United States, where they are being held hostage by the U.S. government as one more way to try to punish the people of Cuba for their refusal to surrender.[2]

---

militia and revolutionary armed forces and police. On April 19 the last invaders surrendered at Playa Girón (Girón Beach), which is the name Cubans use to designate the battle.

2. In September 1998 the FBI announced ten arrests, saying that it had discovered a "Cuban spy network" in Florida. In June 2001, five defendants—Fernando González, René González, Antonio Guerrero, Gerardo Hernández, and Ramón Labañino—were each convicted of "con-

*"The Cuban Revolution that triumphed on January 1, 1959, set an example that revolution is not only necessary, it can be made. It had a powerful and lasting impact on a generation of young workers and students in the U.S. already deeply involved in the spreading mass struggle against Jim Crow segregation."*

**Top:** Detroit, Michigan, April 1961: Picket line called by Fair Play for Cuba Committee protests invasion of Cuba at the Bay of Pigs by 1,500 Cuban-born mercenaries organized and armed by Washington. **Bottom:** Victorious Cuban combatants celebrate defeat of the counterrevolutionary invaders in less than seventy-two hours.

*"For half a century working people of Cuba have held at bay the most powerful empire history has ever known. Today their fighting determination is seen in the five Cuban revolutionaries held hostage in U.S. prisons by Washington to punish the Cuban people for their refusal to surrender."*

**Top:** Cuban militia women prepare to defend the revolution against threatened U.S. military assault during October 1962 "missile crisis." **Bottom:** Demonstration in Washington, D.C., to demand freedom for the Cuban Five, September 2006.

The new edition of *Cuba and the Coming American Revolution* is dedicated to them. To "Gerardo, Ramón, Antonio, Fernando, and René—five exemplary products of the Cuban Revolution who today, even if against their will, serve with honor on the front lines of the class struggle in the United States."

Our deliberations and our actions at the forum here will advance the fight for their freedom.

### A crises-free capitalist world?

Today, above all I want to address my remarks, with all due respect, to those who doubt that socialist revolution in the United States is possible—to those who believe, or fear, that U.S. imperialism is too powerful, and that revolution has become at best a utopian dream.

To those who harbor such doubts, I will pose a question:

What assumptions about the future, explicit or implicit, could justify such a conclusion? What would the future have to look like?

I hope others here will address this as well. But I would like to give my answer.

To reach that conclusion, you would have to believe that the coming decades are going to look more or less like

---

spiracy to act as an unregistered foreign agent." Guerrero, Hernández, and Labañino were also convicted of "conspiracy to commit espionage," and Hernández of "conspiracy to commit murder." Sentences ranged from fifteen years to a double life term plus fifteen years. The five revolutionaries—each of whom has been named "Hero of the Republic of Cuba"—had accepted assignments to keep the Cuban government informed about counterrevolutionary groups in the United States planning terrorist attacks against Cuba. The case of the five has generated a broad international campaign denouncing the harsh conditions of their imprisonment and demanding their release.

those we knew for nearly half a century following World War II.

You would have to believe that there won't again be economic, financial, or social crises on the order of those that marked the first half of the twentieth century. That the ruling families of the imperialist world and their economic wizards have found a way to "manage" capitalism so as to preclude shattering financial crises that could lead to something akin to the Great Depression; to growing assaults on the economic, social, and political rights of the toilers; to spreading imperialist war; to the rise of mass fascist movements in the streets. That such a crisis of the capitalist system would no longer be met by working-class resistance like the mass social movement that exploded in the United States in the 1930s and built the industrial unions.[3]

You would have to be convinced that competition among the imperialist rivals, as well as between them and the more economically advanced semicolonial powers, is diminishing and that their profit rates, which have been on a long downward trend since the mid-1970s, are now going to begin to rise for several decades on an accelerated curve.

You would have to believe that such a turnaround in their accumulation of capital can be accomplished without the massive destruction of productive capacity—human and physical—wrought by decades of war, such as those that culminated in the interimperialist slaughter of World War II. That is what was necessary for the capitalist rulers to get out of the last great depression.

I believe the evidence is overwhelming that the future

---

3. A vivid description of the capitalist social crisis of the 1930s and a case study of the working-class response can be found in the four-volume series by Farrell Dobbs: *Teamster Rebellion, Teamster Power, Teamster Politics*, and *Teamster Bureaucracy*, published by Pathfinder.

*"To conclude that socialist revolution in the U.S. is not possible, you'd have to believe that the ruling families have found a way to 'manage' capitalism so there won't again be world-shaking economic, financial, or social crises."*

Foreclosures on workers' homes continued to mount across the U.S., as employees fled the New York headquarters of Bear Stearns, March 14, 2008, the day the fifth-largest U.S. investment bank collapsed. Within six months, the failure of other top imperialist banks and insurance companies in the U.S. and Europe confirmed not only the worst capitalist financial crisis since the 1930s, but at its roots a deep and accelerating worldwide contraction of industrial production and jobs.

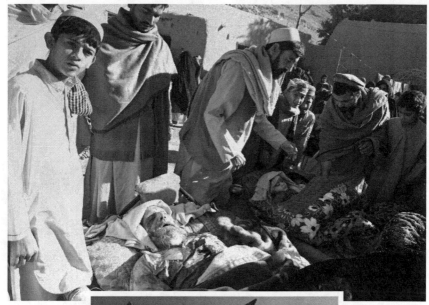

*"The opening guns of World War III are already a decade and a half behind us. We are living through what will be many decades of bloody imperialist wars."*

**Top:** Afghanistan, November 2007. Relatives surround bodies of an elderly man and one of two children killed during U.S.-organized raid on Afghan village.
**Bottom:** Troops of U.S.-led coalition during 1990–91 Gulf War.

we face is the opposite. Just read the headlines this last week! Think about what is happening from Wall Street to Pakistan, from Moscow to Tehran, from the Shanghai stock exchange to the ever-deeper gold mines of South Africa, to the world banking system.

The opening guns of World War III are already a decade and a half *behind* us. We are already living through the opening stages of what will be many decades of bloody wars beginning with ones like those in Iraq, Afghanistan, and Iraq again. That is what the "transformation" of Washington's military structure and strategy is all about.

What is coming are years of economic and financial crises of which the current, still-expanding subprime mortgage crisis—and the even more massive debt balloon it is part of, on and off the balance sheets—offer only a hint.

What is coming are years that will bring increasingly conscious and organized resistance by a growing vanguard of working people pushed to the wall by the bosses' drive to cut wages and increase what they call productivity.

What is coming are years punctuated by street battles with ultrarightist movements aimed against fighting union militants, revolutionary socialists, Blacks, immigrants, Jews, and others—in even the most "stable" of bourgeois democracies.

What is coming are years of economic, social, and political crises and intensifying class struggle that *will* end in World War III, inevitably, *if* the only class that is capable of doing so, the working class, fails to take state power—and thus the power to wage war—out of the hands of the imperialist rulers.

### A fighting working-class vanguard

In the United States, the outlines of these coming battles can already be seen. The historic shift is not ahead of

*"A fighting vanguard of the working class has emerged in action. This is not simply a vanguard of immigrants. This is a working-class vanguard that has developed in response to the employers' antilabor offensive. It is the biggest problem the U.S. rulers face."*

**Above:** Workers' families confront immigration agents after raid on Swift meat processing plant in Greeley, Colorado, December 2006. More than 250 workers were separated from their families and loaded onto planes, with 75 of them deported to Mexico that same day and the rest imprisoned in Texas.

us, it has already occurred.

The most important political development in the United States is something you rarely see images of on your TV screen or read about in the press. Its power has been expressed, however, by the millions of workers who have taken to the streets in cities and towns large and small across the breadth of the country the last two years on May Day, as that historic working-class holiday is fighting to be reborn in the United States as a day of *struggle*.

A fighting vanguard of the working class has emerged in action in the U.S.—taking the rulers by surprise, as registered in their divisions and heated debates over immigration policy. That vanguard is already placing its mark on politics and the class struggle.

This historic shift has increasingly manifested itself in strikes and organizing battles in factories and workplaces from California to Iowa, from Georgia to Utah. Working people, immigrant and U.S.-born, have stood shoulder to shoulder—sometimes in the streets, sometimes inside their factories, and sometimes in front of their neighbors' homes—in face of raids by immigration cops picking off individuals for deportation or on criminal charges of "identity theft" in an attempt to intimidate all. Not just all immigrants, but in fact all workers.

This is not simply an "immigrant" vanguard, although right now it is substantially composed of workers who were born outside the United States, from Mexico and Central America especially. The workers who are helping each other hide from *la migra* in factories, however, and taking in each other's children when their parents are picked up, are not immigrants alone.

This is a *working-class* vanguard. It starts out small relative to the size of the working class as a whole. But it doesn't come out of the blue. It has developed in response to the employers' quarter-century-long antilabor offensive driving down wages and all social benefits, imposing literally life-threatening production speeds, and denying simple dignity to working people on and off the job.

Part of this offensive has been the bosses' oft-times organized efforts to secure themselves an expanding supply of undocumented workers—low-paid and nonunion—simultaneously filling their labor needs and providing a wedge to use in attempting to further divide and stratify the working class. To make each individual worker feel alone and isolated, not part of a powerful and purposeful class.

This is not to paint a rose-colored picture of the class struggle in the United States. My aim is not to convince you that the working class is on the offensive or anything close to that.

To the contrary, it is the employing class that remains on the offensive. Most labor battles end in defeats or, at best, standoffs. The unions—which organize a declining percentage of those working in the United States—increasingly become instruments of the bosses' collaborators in the officialdom. This has been demonstrated once again in the last weeks by the wretched agreements negotiated with the auto industry giants, freeing the employers from responsibility for retirees' future health care needs and capitulating to the bosses' demands for a substantially lower wage scale for new hires working side by side with current employees *doing the very same jobs.*

It's no wonder that today in the U.S. fewer than 7.5 percent of workers in private industry are unionized—down from nearly a third of the private work force half a century ago. And it is going lower.

But none of this is new.

What *is* new, what *is* changing, what *is* of historic impor-

HILDA CUZCO/MILITANT

MILITANT

*"The coming years will be punctuated by street battles with ultrarightist movements that will target fighting union militants, revolutionary socialists, Blacks, immigrants, Jews, and others."*

**Top:** Ultrarightist demonstrators confronting immigrant rights rally in Riverside, New Jersey, August 20, 2006. **Bottom:** Picket line in Los Angeles, 1945, called by unionists and workers organizations against U.S. fascist leader Gerald L.K. Smith.

tance, is the shifting character, composition, and dynamics of the U.S. working class. This is the biggest problem the U.S. rulers face. It is ultimately a bigger crisis for them than Iraq or Afghanistan—because it is more enduring.

The capitalist rulers can, and at some point will, temporarily pull back from any single front in the "global war on terrorism." They can and will make adjustments in their relations with their European rivals, and negotiate tradeoffs with Russia or China. They still have plenty of room to maneuver.

But the working class in the United States, including its expanding immigrant component—some 12 million of whom carry documents not accepted by the cops and courts—is something else. That is the source of the bulk of the capitalists' surplus value, which in turn is the source of their profits, wealth, position, and state power. They utterly depend on this massive pool of superexploited labor. They cannot compete worldwide and accumulate capital without it.

And that fact underlies the increasing confidence, combativity, and politicization of layers within the broad working-class movement in the U.S. today.

The battle to win the vast majority of the working class and the entire labor movement to support the legalization of undocumented immigrants is the single most important "domestic" political question in the United States, and the largest current battle on the road to independent working-class political action, to a labor party based on a militant, fighting union movement.

And it *is* a battle. Many workers—white, Black, Asian, all—are influenced by the virulent anti-immigrant campaign of sections of the ruling class. This is an issue that is determining the future of the labor movement and will continue to do so—much like the fight against Jim Crow segregation did in the 1950s and 1960s, and as the ongoing fight against racism and all forms of discrimination still does.

One of the most crucial fronts of this battle, it should be emphasized, is within the Black community, where the divide-and-rule strategics of the rulers often find an echo—despite the fact that life experience and historical memory prepare the vast majority of African-American workers as natural allies of those fighting for immigrant rights.

Workers in the United States, wherever they were born, face the same class enemy, and determined struggles on any front tend to pull workers together in face of the attempts to divide us. That is what is beginning to happen.

The massive, national, Black-led march on Jena, Louisiana, two months ago by some 20,000 demonstrators—Black, white, Latino and more, native-born and immigrant—protesting the unjust treatment meted out by the courts to six Black teenagers in that town, is a good example of the ways in which the growing proletarian resistance in the United States has already been registered in the strengthening of a broader fighting vanguard. It was the first national action of its size and character in decades in the United States, and the march on Jena was undoubtedly nourished by the power of the recent May Day mobilizations and related actions.

Young Latino workers proudly participating in that action were learning firsthand, and for the first time, of the history of struggles by working people in the United States against Black oppression. And the enthusiastic welcome extended to them by their fellow marchers had a powerful impact on all.

The attempts of the employers to turn immigrant workers—among others—into scapegoats in order to guarantee the availability of a pool of superexploited labor will not cease. Any sharp economic crisis will intensify the battle for the political soul of the working class on this and other questions.

Unlike previous periods in U.S. history, however, when the rulers were successful in radically dividing working people along lines of race and national origin—as in the aftermath of the defeat of Radical Reconstruction following the Civil War, or after World War I—it is precisely the unprecedented internationalization of labor, the vast scope of working-class migration, dwarfing the great waves of the nineteenth and early twentieth centuries, that is today one of our greatest strengths.

We learn from the traditions of struggle coming together from all parts of the world. As we fight shoulder to shoulder, it becomes harder for the bosses to pit "us" against "them." It becomes more possible to see that our class interests are not the same as those of "our" bosses, "our" government, or "our" two parties.

### Revolutionary continuity

As decades of deepening crises and intensifying class struggle open ahead of us, we have something else in our favor. The revolutionary potential of the great radicalization in the 1930s was squandered and diverted into support for capitalism's "New Deal" and then its inevitable accompaniment, the "War Deal"—the imperialist slaughter of World War II.

It was the resources and attraction of a powerful bureaucratic social caste in the USSR camouflaging itself as a communist leadership on a world scale that made this possible. Today, however, that enormous political obstacle no longer stands across the road toward independent working-class political action and revolutionary socialist leadership. Imperialism can no longer rely on it as an

*"As struggles by working people deepen, new generations of vanguard fighters the world over will search for historical experiences from which they can learn not only how to fight, but how to fight to win. The lessons of the Russian and Cuban revolutions will be sought after once again."*

**Top:** Soldier speaks to a council ("soviet") of soldiers and sailors during 1917 Russian Revolution. In October 1917 the working class, led by the Bolshevik Party, overthrew the regime of the capitalists and landlords, and the soviets of workers, peasants, and soldiers became the new government. **Bottom:** Books and pamphlets recording lessons of more than 150 years of revolutionary working-class struggle worldwide were available at the Pathfinder booth at Venezuela book fair, November 2007.

enforcer of peaceful coexistence, of "spheres of influence" around the globe. And the most combative and courageous leaders of working-class battles, of national liberation movements, of radicalizing youth, will no longer be drawn toward that Stalinist negation of everything Marx and Engels and Lenin fought for, falsely believing it is communism.

The lessons of the Russian Revolution and the Communist International under Lenin will be sought after once again as new generations of vanguard fighters search for historical experiences from which they can learn not only how to fight but how to fight *to win*.

That is why, as these battles politically deepen, the real history of the Cuban Revolution too will again be increasingly sought after.

Why has the Cuban Revolution followed a completely different course the last twenty years, salvaging and fortifying its socialist revolution, as the bureaucratic regimes of Eastern Europe and the Soviet Union—which many falsely thought Cuba resembled—imploded?

How has it been possible for the Cuban people to hold at bay the most powerful empire history has ever known—or ever will know—for almost fifty years?

Why to this day, despite decades of struggle throughout the hemisphere, does Cuba remain the only free territory of the Americas?

To state that fact is not to diminish the importance of the space that has been conquered by the people of Venezuela these last years, nor the new ground still being taken in struggle. It simply registers the indisputable fact that what will be Venezuela's January 1 lies ahead of us, not behind. That what will be the challenge of a Playa Girón for the Venezuelan toilers lies ahead of us, not behind.

It is in search of answers to these burning questions that

books such as *The First and Second Declarations of Havana* being presented here at this book fair by Pathfinder Press,[4] and *Our History Is Still Being Written: The Story of Three Chinese-Cuban Generals in the Cuban Revolution,* are read worldwide with such great interest. Yes, socialist revolution is possible. It can be defended. It can be advanced even in face of our most powerful enemies.

As the Cuban people have proven in practice, a better world is indeed possible. But in any radical or enduring manner, only through socialist revolution.

The stakes posed in the questions we are discussing here at this forum are immeasurable. We confront not only the destruction of the health, welfare, and environment of the earth and all toiling humanity—the destruction of land and labor, the wellsprings of all human progress and culture. Those are and will be the inevitable, devastating consequences of the workings of capitalism. The limits we can impose on those consequences are and can only be a by-product of our revolutionary struggle. And should we fail, we can be sure that we all ultimately face a future of nuclear devastation as well.

Every revolutionary struggle, anywhere in the world— not least important right here in Venezuela—is a vital piece of the international battle. But until power is taken from Washington's hands by the workers and farmers, and

---

4. Well-attended book presentations were held at the 2007 fair on *Cuba and the Coming American Revolution* by Jack Barnes, *The First and Second Declarations of Havana, Malcolm X Talks to Young People,* and two books by Thomas Sankara: *We Are Heirs of the World's Revolutions* and *Women's Liberation and the African Freedom Struggle. Our History Is Still Being Written* had a similar reception at the previous Venezuela book fair a year earlier. These and hundreds of other Pathfinder titles in Spanish, English, and other languages were available to participants in the Caracas book fair.

Yankee imperialism is thus decisively disarmed, nothing lasting is settled.

That is why it is no small matter to answer: Yes, revolution is not only possible in the United States, it is coming. Yes, revolutionary struggles are on the agenda—but their outcome depends on us. Yes, fighting shoulder to shoulder with others determined to triumph along this course is the most meaningful life possible.

# 'The class battles ahead are inevitable, their outcome is not. That depends on us.'

## by Mary-Alice Waters

First, a thank you to all the panelists for their remarks—to José [González] from the ALBA Cultural Fund, Erick [Rangel] from the national leadership team of the United Socialist Party of Venezuela youth, and Carolina [Álvarez], editorial director of Monte Ávila.

On behalf of Pathfinder Press, I above all want to express our appreciation to Monte Ávila for the decision—described by Carolina—to publish *Is Socialist Revolution in the U.S. Possible?* in not one but two editions for the 2008 Venezuela International Book Fair. One edition to be distributed free to book fair participants here tomorrow, and the other to be sold across the country over the coming

---

*The following talk was given in Caracas, Venezuela, as part of a November 14, 2008, panel launching a Spanish-language edition of* Is Socialist Revolution in the U.S. Possible? *released that week by the Venezuelan publisher Monte Ávila. The event, held during the fourth Venezuela International Book Fair, was jointly sponsored by Monte Ávila and Pathfinder Press.*

year through the Librerías del Sur chain of bookstores.

I also want to thank CENAL (National Book Center), the organizer of the Venezuela International Book Fair, for the important initiative its national leadership took last year in organizing the fair's Central Forum on the theme, "The United States: A possible revolution." As you have already learned, that was the origin of the talk that is at the center of the booklet Pathfinder and Monte Ávila are jointly presenting here.

It is not by accident that one of the leading daily newspapers in the United States, the *New York Times*, just this week disparagingly singled out that forum by name as an example of how divorced from reality all you here in Venezuela are. How divorced from reality all revolutionary-minded workers are, everywhere. That we should even think such a ridiculous proposition worth discussing! That we should think events like the Venezuela International Book Fair, events that promote reading and culture and civil debate among working people, point a way forward for humanity.

As we said last year, however, the question of whether socialist revolution is possible in the United States is no small matter. Its "answer, in practice, will ultimately determine the future of humanity—or more accurately, perhaps, whether there is a future for humanity."

**A way to 'manage' capitalism?**

What most struck me in rereading last year's presentation was the list of assumptions one would have to make to reach the conclusion that socialist revolution in the U.S. is *not* possible. And then thinking about what has transpired in the world in the last twelve months!

"To reach that conclusion," we said, "you would have to believe that there won't again be economic, financial, or social crises on the order of those that marked the first

cuento "El caballero" el Primer Premio en el Concurso Anual de Cuentos convocado por el diario El Nacional de Caracas. Su novela: Los hijos, obtuvo el Segundo Premio Latinoamericano "Casa de Las Américas"- (Caracas, 1962). En cuento: Llegada de todos los trenes del mundo (Cuenca, 1932).

MICHAEL BAUMANN/MILITANT

MICHAEL BAUMANN/MILITANT

*"The class battles ahead of us are inevitable, but their outcome is not. That depends on us. On our capacity to face the truth and speak with clarity to fellow combatants, to learn to rely on our own class solidarity and unity in struggle."*

**Top:** Panel at Nov. 2008 presentation of *Is Socialist Revolution in the U.S. Possible?* Left to right: Erick Rangel, student and youth leader of United Socialist Party of Venezuela; Mary-Alice Waters; Carolina Álvarez, editorial director of Monte Ávila publishing house; and José González, president of ALBA Cultural Fund. **Bottom:** A lively discussion followed the presentations. **Inset:** Cover of Monte Ávila edition distributed at book fair.

half of the twentieth century. That the ruling families of the imperialist world and their economic wizards have found a way to 'manage' capitalism so as to preclude shattering financial crises that could lead to something akin to the Great Depression. . . .

"You would have to be convinced that competition among the imperialist rivals, as well as between them and the more economically advanced semicolonial powers, is diminishing and that their profit rates . . . are now going to begin to rise for several decades on an accelerated curve."

A year ago when we were discussing these questions here in Caracas, the main U.S. stock market index, just a few weeks earlier, had closed at its all-time high of a little over 14,000. Yesterday it swung wildly by almost a thousand points, from under 8,000—more than 40 percent below its peak—to close at almost 9,000. These manic fluctuations have become so much a daily occurrence as to become commonplace. And everyone knows they simply announce another plunge. Trillions of dollars of what Marx called "fictitious capital" have disappeared in the last year, and the bottom is nowhere in sight—nowhere.

What seemingly started as a capitalist crisis centered in credit and banking has now been revealed to be something of a very different dimension. As the de facto bankruptcy of General Motors bears witness, the deepest contraction of industrial production and employment since the opening decades of the last century is accelerating dramatically. And the inevitability of such a contraction has underlaid this worldwide crisis from the beginning.

It is worth reminding ourselves that the Great Depression of the 1930s was not the consequence of the stock market crash of 1929 and subsequent banking crises alone. Its roots are found in the violently intensifying competition among capitalist powers in the years leading up to

World War I—for colonial possessions, access to markets and raw materials, and inexpensive sources of labor to exploit—and the economic and social breakdowns and financial catastrophe that accompanied that interimperialist slaughter and its aftermath. And it took the global carnage of the Second World War, including its massive physical destruction of capital across Europe and Asia from 1939 to 1945, to lay the basis for the exploiting classes to pull out of that crisis.

That is important. As Lenin stressed, there is no hopeless situation for capitalism. The two decades from 1930 to 1950 showed once again that the finance capitalists, if they are not stopped beforehand, can dig themselves out of any crisis—by inflicting enough bloody defeats on the working classes and destroying enough of the world's existing industrial capacity.

The only question is the price the toilers will be made to pay.

The only solution is taking the power to inflict these horrors—state power—out of their hands, once and for all.

**The road forced upon us**

Is that possible? That is, after all, the question we posed a year ago. And we made the point that revolutionary struggles by the toilers are not only inevitable, they will be initiated at first not by us, "but forced upon us by the crisis-driven assaults of the propertied classes."

The working class in massive numbers never enters on the road of revolutionary struggle lightly, or all at once. Workers sense the stakes, the sacrifices it will entail, the uncertainty. Our class in its majority exhausts other alternatives first, including alternatives to communist political leadership.

AP PHOTO/KATHY WILLENS

JORGE LERTORA/MILITANT

*"Revolutionary struggle by the toilers will be forced upon us by the crisis-driven assaults of the propertied rulers."*

**Top:** With unemployment rising sharply, jobless workers line up outside job fair in New York City, November 2008. **Bottom:** Some 1,500 people of many nationalities joined July 2008 march and rally against immigration raid at Agriprocessors meatpacking plant in Postville, Iowa. The protest was led off by women workers (one of them with bullhorn) displaying electronic ankle "bracelets" they are being forced to wear by federal immigration cops.

Earlier this month, for example, tens of millions of workers in the United States cast their ballots for Barack Obama, the presidential candidate of one of the two dominant ruling parties of the greatest imperialist empire ever. But one must be blind to history to think that the chief executive-elect of what Marx and Engels called the "committee for managing the common affairs of the whole bourgeoisie" can or wants to do anything other than serve the interests of the U.S. capitalist class. The interests of the propertied rulers who cold-bloodedly selected him as the best man for the job right now.

Even before the new stage of the global retrenchment that is now accelerating, however, we have already seen, already been part of, the opening skirmishes of a fighting vanguard of the working class emerging in the United States. We saw this vanguard-in-becoming as millions of workers took to the streets of cities and towns across the country in 2006 and 2007 to demand the legalization of some 12 million immigrants whose documents the U.S. government does not recognize. They retook May Day as a fighting holiday of the working class.

We saw it earlier this year in the defiant response of workers across the Midwest—both immigrant and U.S.-born—to police raids on factories and homes, the roundups and deportations of thousands of workers, the criminal charges of "identity theft" brought against hundreds. That fighting response was captured most dramatically by the women, together with their children, who led the protest marches, proudly displaying the electronic police monitors shackled around their ankles. It was registered by the workers of all nationalities who joined them.

This is a working-class vanguard strengthened by its increasingly international character, by the traditions of struggle being added by workers from around the world to the longtime traditions of working-class battles in the United States itself. This is a working class that is slowly but surely learning in struggle the life-or-death necessity of fighting shoulder to shoulder—as well as how to do so.

The rapidly escalating economic and social crisis has only barely begun to be felt by working people, whether in the United States or internationally. While home foreclosures have been climbing over the past year, reaching more than one million in 2008 alone, it is only in the last months that the factory closings and layoffs have begun to accelerate.

Just last week the DHL courier service shut down domestic service in North America, a move that will result in the layoff of more than 7,000 workers in the industrial belt of southern Ohio, with spreading repercussions for working people from Cincinnati to Dayton to Columbus. This year General Motors and other automobile companies have pushed thousands onto the streets, and thousands more auto and auto parts workers all over the country, and indeed all over the world, will follow in the months ahead—regardless of whether or not GM or Chrysler or both file for bankruptcy in the near future. Yahoo, the internet company, is laying off 10 percent of its workforce worldwide. Monster banks are slashing their workforces. And you can multiply those examples manyfold.

The majority—both in the United States and beyond, including here in Venezuela—still live with the grim hope that maybe the slump really won't get so bad, perhaps its worst possibilities will bypass our lands. But world capitalism in crisis will not spare the most vulnerable.

### A fight for political clarity

I want to close by emphasizing one point.

Our job today is above all a political one. While the

class battles ahead of us are inevitable, their outcome is not. That depends on us. On our capacity to unflinchingly face the truth and speak with clarity to fellow combatants, to learn to rely on our own increasing class solidarity and unity in struggle. To understand, and help other vanguard fighters to understand, that the driving force of all history since the dawn of recorded time has been class struggle, not conspiracies. That the poisons of Jew-hatred and racism rob us of our ability to see that the real problem is the capitalist system itself, and that the real enemy we must defeat is the propertied classes whose wealth and power depend on that system.

Working people the world over are in for decades of intertwined economic, military, social, and political crises, and accompanying explosive class battles. The period we are entering will be more akin to the years from the opening of the twentieth century through World War II than to anything any of us have lived through. The one thing we can be sure of is that our side, our class, will have more than one opportunity to alter the course of history in the only way we can—the way the workers and farmers of Cuba did it fifty years ago, and the way the working people of the tsarist empire did it four decades before them.

That's why the continuing example of the Cuban Revolution is so important today. And, I would add, it's why the fight to free the five heroes of the Cuban Revolution—who, against their will and ours, have been serving on the front lines of the class struggle in the United States for more than ten years now—is an international battle of the first order.

All these are among the real questions in front of us. For the opportunity to address them, and to join in the debate over them, both this year and last, we express our thanks, our respect, and our class solidarity.

*"The book fair was marked by the resources the Venezuelan government is devoting to the expansion of literacy and popular access to culture."*

2007 book fair. **Top:** Dance performance. **Bottom:** Fairgoers browse hundreds of titles by Venezuelan publishers in main tent.

# Prospects for revolution in the U.S.
# A necessary debate

*by Olympia Newton*

## I

CARACAS, Venezuela—The first two days of the November 9–18 Third Venezuela International Book Fair have been marked by the expansion of literacy and popular access to culture in this country, as well as political debate sparked by the fair's theme, "The United States: a possible revolution."

A wide variety of books are for sale—from poetry collections to histories of the struggles against Spanish colonial rule in South America, from cookbooks to titles on the place of the Cuban Revolution in the world today. Nearly 800 book presentations and artists' performances offer a place for working people and others to discuss literature,

*These articles reporting on the forum "The United States: a possible revolution" appeared in the November 26 and December 3, 2007, issues of the* Militant, *a socialist newsweekly.*

the arts, and politics. Almost 200 publishing houses are participating.

"The rebirth of culture being celebrated here is especially significant considering all the books and bookstores that were burned during the years of the dictatorships in our countries," Alicia Castro, Argentina's ambassador to Venezuela, said at the opening ceremony. She was referring to the brutal military regimes that dominated much of Latin America during parts of the 1960s and '70s. Argentina, which from 1976 to 1983 endured one of the most murderous of those tyrannies, is the country of honor at this year's fair.

Reflecting the Venezuelan government's programs to preserve the languages and cultures of indigenous peoples, the inaugural ceremony was kicked off by a children's choir that sang the national anthem in the language of the Anu people. Minister of Culture Francisco Sesto and Vice President Jorge Rodríguez were the featured speakers. Rodríguez described the expansion of publishing and book distribution in Venezuela in recent years, and the literacy campaign that has taught more than one million workers and peasants to read and write.

### 'United States: a possible revolution'

Ramón Medero, president of the National Book Center (CENAL), welcomed participation in the fair by many individuals active in a variety of social movements, especially those coming from the United States. He also introduced the fair's theme, "The United States: a possible revolution." Noting that the fair's central activity is a five-day rolling forum on that topic, Medero pointed to the importance of the fact that participants will be discussing and affirming "not just whether a revolution is necessary in North America, but that it is possible."

The week-long discussion featured twenty-two panelists, mostly political activists and writers from the United States, as well as a number of U.S. citizens living in Venezuela.[5] Four or five of them spoke each day, debating diverse political views. Hundreds of Venezuelans and others took part in one or more sessions, with dozens raising questions and making comments from the floor. The forum was covered by Venezuelan television, radio, and newspapers. The issues debated on the character of the working class and prospects for revolution in the United States sparked a political discussion that permeated the book fair.

The forum's opening session, attended by 150 people, was November 10. The panelists at the morning session were Mary-Alice Waters, a member of the Socialist Workers Party National Committee and president of Pathfinder Press, and Eva Golinger, a Venezuelan-American lawyer and author of *The Chávez Code* and *Bush vs. Chávez*.

The afternoon panelists were U.S.-born journalist Chris Carlson, a regular contributor to the website www.venezuelaanalysis.com, and Tufara Waller, coordinator of the cultural program of the Highlander Center in Tennessee and director of the We Shall Overcome project. Their remarks

---

5. In addition to panelists mentioned in this account, others included Charles Hardy, a former Maryknoll priest who has lived in Venezuela for many years; University of Minnesota political science professor August Nimtz; former University of Colorado professor Ward Churchill; Dada Maheshvarananda, a U.S.-born activist, writer, and monk living in Caracas; and William Blum, a writer on the history of CIA operations.

Some speakers invited to take part in the forum were unable to make it during that event, but joined the discussion in the following days. A November 17 program featured Kathleen Cleaver, former national spokesperson for the Black Panther Party. A video interview with Noam Chomsky, the author, anarchist, and linguistics professor, was played after the conclusion of the forum, and a booklet containing a translation of his comments was distributed.

and the subsequent discussion from the floor opened a debate on several of the most sharply contested issues.

"I am speaking here today as one of a small minority, including among those who call themselves leftists, or revolutionaries, a minority that says without hesitation or qualification: Yes, a revolution *is* possible in the United States. Socialist revolution," said Waters, the opening speaker. "What's more, revolutionary *struggle* by the toilers along the path I just described is *inevitable*. It will be initiated at first not by the toilers, but forced upon us by the crisis-driven assaults of the propertied classes."

Waters said she was addressing those who consider socialist revolution in the United States to be impossible, "a utopian dream." Such a conclusion, she said, has to rest on the assumption "that the coming decades are going to look more or less like those we knew for nearly half a century following World War II."

"You would have to be convinced that competition among the imperialist rivals, as well as between them and the more economically advanced semicolonial powers, is diminishing and profit rates, which have been on a long downward trend since the mid-1970s, are now going to begin to rise for several decades on an accelerated curve," she said. "That such a turnaround in their accumulation of capital can be accomplished without the massive destruction of productive capacity—human and physical—wrought by decades of war, such as those that culminated in the interimperialist slaughter of World War II. That is what was necessary for the capitalist rulers to get out of the last great depression."

**Developing working-class vanguard**

The economic crisis of capitalism drives the bosses' offensive against the working class in the United States, Waters said, and these assaults are generating resistance. She

*"The battle to win the vast majority of the working class and labor movement to support legalization of immigrants is the single most important 'domestic' political question in the U.S. It will determine the future of the labor movement."*

**Top:** May 1, 2007, march in Chicago of 150,000 demanding legalization of all immigrants. **Bottom:** September 2007 protest of 20,000 against anti-Black bigotry in Jena, Lousiana, demands justice for the Jena 6. The welcome received by participating immigrant workers from Central America dealt a blow to prejudices used by the bosses to divide and weaken the working-class movement.

pointed to the mass street mobilizations on May Day the last two years demanding legalization for undocumented immigrants as evidence of the beginning development of a working-class vanguard.

She said the mobilization of tens of thousands against racist injustice at the hands of the cops and courts in Jena, Louisiana, in September was "the first national action of its size and character in decades" and "was undoubtedly nourished by the power of the recent May Day mobilizations."

In this context, Waters said, "The lessons of the Russian Revolution and the Communist International under Lenin will be sought after once again," as will the real history of the Cuban Revolution, "as new generations of vanguard fighters search for historical experiences from which they can learn not only how to fight but how to fight *to win*."

"How has it been possible," she said, "for the Cuban people to hold at bay the most powerful empire history has ever known—or ever will know—for almost fifty years? Why to this day, despite decades of struggle throughout the Americas, does Cuba remain the only free territory of the Americas?"

In her remarks Golinger said, "I have to disagree that Cuba is the only free territory of the Americas. Because here in Venezuela we are also free, or we are in the process of freeing ourselves." She predicted that the government-supported package of constitutional amendments will pass in a December 2 referendum here despite a campaign by the pro-imperialist opposition, and pointed to this as an example of how "we are freeing ourselves with the enemy living in the same house." [6]

---

6. The December 2, 2007, referendum on a package of sixty-nine constitutional amendments was defeated by a 51–49 percent margin, with a high abstention rate.

Golinger also said she didn't "share the same optimism that a revolution is possible in the United States." Golinger, who has lived in Venezuela since 1999, said that in preparing for the book fair she had spoken "with Noam Chomsky about how the process of change will have to be very slow in such a capitalist consumer society."

People in the United States are deadened to conditions of suffering, Golinger said, because "it's very easy to change the channel. People are not poor or hungry in the U.S. like they were in Venezuela. You get two or three credit cards in the mail every day. There is poverty, but it's only in a few small sectors."

As for the movement for legalization of immigrants, Golinger said, "Even though they were demanding to be recognized, it was to live inside a capitalist consumer society.

"The only way to achieve structural change in the United States is to make advances here" in Venezuela, she said. "Then we can go there and say, 'Look at the Bolivarian Revolution, what we've accomplished. You can do the same.'"

### Issues are joined

The two presentations were followed by a lively discussion, and the issues presented on the opening day have been hotly contested at other book fair activities, too. Golinger's remarks reflect widely held opinions here that there is little hope for revolutionary change in the United States.

The majority of those speaking during the first round of discussion at the central forum expressed doubts at such a possibility. Several Venezuelan speakers said in various ways that living standards in the United States are too high for there to be resistance, or that people are brainwashed by capitalist-owned media.

Some participants from the United States offered a dif-

*"The stakes posed in the questions we are discussing are immeasurable. Until power is taken from Washington's hands by the workers and farmers and Yankee imperialism is decisively disarmed, nothing lasting is settled."*

Panelists and audience joined the issues during the five-day exchange on "The United States: a possible revolution." **Top:** Participant speaks from floor. At speakers' table, from left: former Maryknoll priest Charles Hardy; Bernardo Alvarez Herrera, Venezuela's ambassador to U.S.; moderator José González Fernández-Larrera, president of the ALBA Cultural Fund; University of Minnesota professor August Nimtz. **Bottom left:** Tufara Waller, director of cultural program at Highlander Center in Tennessee. **Bottom right:** Chris Carlson, U.S. journalist living in Venezuela; Luis Bilbao, moderator.

ferent view. "I don't consider myself to have been turned into an idiot," said Diógenes Abreu, a Dominican-born activist living in New York. "Nor do I consider the millions who live in the United States who oppose its policies to be idiots.

"But I also don't share all the optimism of Mary-Alice," Abreu said. "If, as she pointed out, fewer than 7.5 percent of private-sector workers are organized, and the working class has to be in the leadership of a revolution, how can you say it's possible sooner rather than later?"

"The people I work with have never read Noam Chomsky," said Tufara Waller from the Highlander Center. Pointing to working people in New Orleans still confronting the social disaster in the wake of Hurricane Katrina, as well as tobacco farmers in North Carolina fighting to keep their land, she noted, "They are people who are hungry, who understand that they have to fight to live." And many people in the United States don't have credit cards, either, Waller added.

### Two-party system

The discussion continued in the afternoon, kicked off by Waller and Chris Carlson. Originally from Colorado, Carlson has lived in Venezuela for the last three years.

"Many Venezuelans, including President Chávez, say that Bush is the problem," he said. "But Bush is not the problem. He is just a product of a system dominated by big corporations." Carlson used a PowerPoint presentation to document that both the Democratic and Republican parties in the United States are financed by the same major corporations.

Contenders for the Democratic and Republican party nominations for the 2008 presidential elections, Carlson said, present fundamentally the same perspectives: driving ahead with the war in Iraq, and maintaining the economic embargo against Cuba and hostility toward Venezuela. The candidates are now debating health care, he said, but none has any proposal other than to keep health care a money-making institution at the expense of the well-being of millions.

Waller described the history of the Highlander Center and its current projects to organize against environmental degradation, intolerable working conditions, and racist discrimination.

"If both parties are so dominated by the monopolies, why don't people rise up against them?" a Venezuelan participant asked Carlson. Referring to the idea often heard in left-wing circles in the United States that the 2000 election was stolen by Bush supporters in Florida, Carlson said the majority of people in the United States don't see it that way and "consider the Bush administration a legitimate government."

A young Venezuelan who just returned after living in the United States also took the floor during the discussion. He described the school he attended in a working-class area of Alabama. "The education system there is not about learning at all," he said. The young people he went to school with wanted to change society but didn't know how to begin.

"This forum is only the beginning of what will be several days of discussion on these themes," said program moderator Luis Bilbao, an Argentine-born journalist, at the conclusion of the first day.

II

Among the issues discussed at the five-day forum, the sharpest debate focused, first, on the impact and importance of millions of Latin American immigrant workers in the United States. And, second, on the history of revolutionary struggles of working people in the United States and the lessons of those struggles for revolutionary perspectives. In a striking way, the discussion registered that those living and engaged in the class struggle in the United States generally expressed greater confidence in the revolutionary capacities of working people there than did those—both U.S. citizens and Latin American participants—living outside the United States.

Several panelists are active in work to expand rights for immigrants in the United States. These included Diógenes Abreu, a Dominican-born community organizer who currently lives in New York; Luis Rodríguez, a Chicano activist in California's San Fernando Valley; and Gustavo Torres, an organizer for the immigrant rights group Casa de Maryland. Several of them gave vivid and accurate pictures of conditions of life for immigrant workers in the United States and the growing resistance and confidence manifested in strikes and ongoing street mobilizations against raids and deportations.

Both Torres and Antonio González, president of the Southwest Voter Education and Registration Project, said the road to "empowerment" is organizing Latinos to vote. "What does a revolutionary do in the U.S. today?" asked González. "Take power wherever you can" by electing Latinos to city, state, and federal offices. The graphs he projected for all to see depicted the growing number of Latino voters and officeholders.

During the discussion periods day after day, a number of participants from Venezuela and elsewhere in Latin America took exception to the evidence that immigrant workers resisting the superexploitation they face in the United States are an important force in the working-class vanguard that is emerging there. In various ways, several said that Latin Americans living and working in the United States are simply there to get "a piece of the pie."

"They are only there to get passports," said one participant. "Once they get them they'll stop marching." Many spoke with barely concealed contempt for immigrant workers as sellouts who have bought into the "American dream" instead of remaining in Latin America to fight for political, economic, and social change.

In the discussion, Carlos Samaniego, a packinghouse worker from Minnesota, countered this view. He described the vanguard role that immigrant workers are playing in struggles in the United States—from coal mines in the West to union struggles in Midwest slaughterhouses.

**America's revolutionary heritage**

The other hotly debated question was the revolutionary history of toilers in the United States and, by extension, prospects for a third American revolution, a socialist revolution.

"America was created by revolution," said panelist Lee Sustar, labor editor of the *Socialist Worker* newspaper, which reflects the views of the International Socialist Organization. Speaking at the November 13 session, he referred to the U.S. Civil War as "the completion of the bourgeois-democratic revolution" that had won independence for the thirteen British colonies some eighty years earlier.

"There has never been a revolution in the United States, and anyone who thinks there has been is ignorant of their own history," responded panelist Richard Gott, a British author and journalist. Gott said the American Revolution, which defeated British colonial rule, could not be considered a revolution. Rather, it was a war to take land from Native American tribes, whose territory, he said, was be-

*"There has never been a revolution in the United States and never will be!" asserted one participant. The revolutionary history of toilers in the U.S. and prospects for a third American revolution, a socialist revolution, were hotly debated at Caracas forum.*

**Top:** Black troops, most of them freed slaves, during the Civil War of 1861–65, the second American revolution. **Bottom:** Federal troops destroy railroad tracks in Georgia during Union Army's "March to the Sea" led by Gen. William T. Sherman, 1864. The offensive cut the Confederacy in two and helped break the back of the slavocracy.

ing protected by the British royal army.

"No, a revolution is not possible in the United States," said Gott. "It is conservative and reactionary. The only hope is Latin America."

"I want to express my total agreement," interjected Haiman El Troudi, the moderator of the panel that day. "There never has been a revolution in the United States and never will be!" El Troudi has held several offices in the Chávez government and written books including *Being Capitalist Is Bad Business* and *History of the Bolivarian Revolution*.

"It is impossible for a revolution to begin in the United States," said a Venezuelan participant from the floor. He pointed to what he considered U.S. workers' complicity with Washington's wars against Iraq and Afghanistan as proof that working people there are desensitized to injustice.

But in remarks during the November 11 panel, ex-Marine and founder of Iraq Veterans Against the War Jimmy Massey described his own evolution from a prowar patriot to a staunch opponent of the war in Iraq. He walked through day-to-day experiences in Iraq that led him to oppose U.S. policies in the Middle East and to organize fellow soldiers to do the same.

Another idea frequently expressed by speakers from the floor and by a few panelists was that "change has to come from the South," referring primarily to Latin America. Many said the only hope was to wait until enough countries in Latin America close their doors to imperialist penetration so as to cause a collapse in the U.S. economy. The fact that nowhere in Latin America but Cuba have working people yet successfully carried through to victory the kind of revolutionary struggle necessary to end imperialist domination was largely absent from that picture.

Some participants argued that U.S. capitalism would be thrown into crisis if enough leftist governments were elected in Latin America and refused to sign bilateral "free-trade" agreements with Washington or join the U.S.-initiated Free Trade Area of the Americas. Others pointed to popular struggles in Venezuela, Ecuador, Bolivia, and Nicaragua as being the key to educating working people in the United States. Despite different arguments and emphases, the point of agreement was that no initiative could be expected from working people inside the imperialist bastion.

A contrasting point of view was presented by Héctor Pesquera, a leader of the Hostosiano Independence Movement of Puerto Rico. "The Puerto Rican struggle is connected to the North American revolution," he said. Pesquera summarized the worsening conditions facing both working people in Puerto Rico and Puerto Ricans living in New York. Pointing to the movement that forced Washington to withdraw its naval base from the Puerto Rican island of Vieques, Pesquera noted that this blow to the U.S. rulers had strengthened social movements in the United States.

"I'm going to take issue with what every one of you has said," stated Amiri Baraka, a writer from Newark, New Jersey, speaking from the audience. Baraka, a panelist on the closing day of the event, has been active in Black nationalist, Maoist, and Democratic Party politics since the 1960s. Attacking Sustar for not identifying himself as a "Trotskyite," and falsely accusing panelist George Katsiaficas of having introduced himself as a former member of the Black Panthers, Baraka's intervention was the first time in four days of sharp debate that the tone of civil discourse was breached.

### Final session

"When I first heard the theme of this forum, I thought it was a joke," said Steve Brouwer, an American living in

Venezuela and writing a book on peasant cooperatives. Brouwer was a panelist at the final session. "But the more I thought about what is happening in the world, the more I listened to my Latino brothers here, the more I became convinced that revolutionary change in the U.S. *is* possible."

Brouwer said that working-class complacency in the United States in the 1920s had given way to labor battles in the 1930s that shaped U.S. politics for forty-five years. He cited a "mildly progressive" Democratic Party, influenced by these developments in the labor movement, as key to what he called a progressive course that ended with the election of Ronald Reagan in 1980.

Amiri Baraka and Amina Baraka were also panelists at the final session.

Amina Baraka, introducing herself as "a Black woman who is a communist who uses the cultural arena," spoke about her work and read a poem.

Amiri Baraka came back to the previous day's discussion, disagreeing with Gott and others who denied there have been two great revolutions in U.S. history. He also disagreed with Sustar's characterization of the Civil War as the completion of the bourgeois-democratic revolution.

"That revolution has never been completed," Baraka said. "There is still no democracy for Blacks." He proposed that Blacks and Latinos, including a layer of the Black bourgeoisie, unite around a program to abolish the electoral college; establish a unicameral parliamentary system; ban "private money" from election campaigns; make voting compulsory; and restore voting rights to felons. Such constitutional reforms, he said, would shift power towards "people's democracy" in the United States. Revolutionary goals could then be put on the agenda.

What has derailed all previous revolutionary struggles

in the United States, Baraka argued, is "white privilege." He cited the defeat of Radical Reconstruction following the Civil War, the failure of the 1930s labor upsurge to go further, and the decline of the mass movement that brought down Jim Crow segregation as three examples. Moreover, "white privilege" and the failure of the "white left" to fight it remain the primary obstacle to struggles today.

Baraka also renewed his attack on Katsiaficas, who as part of the panel the previous day had spoken about Asian student struggles. Baraka accused him of being an agent who had selected that topic in order to try to stir up support in Venezuela for student marches against the government of Hugo Chávez.

Baraka concluded by reading "Somebody Blew Up America," a Spanish translation of which was distributed to participants. Written by Baraka after September 11, 2001, the verse presents a long list of historical atrocities, interlacing anti-imperialist and anticapitalist rhetoric with conspiracy theories of history and anti-Semitism. "Who decide Jesus get crucified," the poem asks. "Who knew the World Trade Center was gonna get bombed / Who told 4000 Israeli workers at the Twin Towers / To stay home that day / Why did Sharon stay away?"

During the opening day of the panel, a participant from Panama had said during the discussion that Jews are the main problem facing working people in the world today because "they have all the money" and control everything. Norton Sandler, a member of the Socialist Workers Party in the United States, spoke from the floor the next day and pointed to the deadly danger scapegoating and Jew-hatred posed for the working-class movement.

After Baraka's remarks the final day, Mary-Alice Waters took the floor to thank the organizers of the book fair "for bringing together diverse forces with such a broad variety of views for the discussion that took place here." She stressed the importance of civil debate, noting that "the poison of agent- and race-baiting must be condemned by all."

At the close of the five-day forum, Ramón Medero, president of Venezuela's National Book Center, the sponsor of the fair, expressed his appreciation to all the panelists whose efforts had contributed to the success of the event, and satisfaction that the fair served to open a much-needed political discussion.

# INDEX

**"T**here will be a victorious revolution in the United States before a victorious counterrevolution in Cuba."

—Fidel Castro, March 1961

# Cuba and the Coming American Revolution

Jack Barnes

That bold assertion remains as timely today as when the words were spoken nearly fifty years ago on the eve of Washington's ignominious defeat at the Bay of Pigs.

This book is about the struggles of working people in the imperialist heartland, the youth who are attracted to them, and the example set by the people of Cuba that revolution is not only necessary—it can be made. It is about the class struggle in the United States, where the political capacities and revolutionary potential of workers and farmers are today as utterly discounted by the ruling powers as were those of the Cuban toilers. And just as wrongly.

*Second edition, with a new foreword by Mary-Alice Waters. $10*

# The Russian Revolution

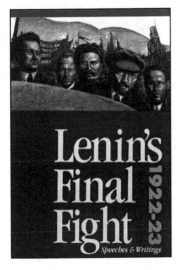

## Lenin's Final Fight
### Speeches and Writings, 1922–23
**V.I. LENIN**

In the early 1920s Lenin waged a political battle in the Communist Party leadership in the USSR to maintain the course that had enabled workers and peasants to overthrow the tsarist empire, carry out the first socialist revolution, and begin building a world communist movement. The issues posed in this fight—from the leadership's class composition, to the worker-peasant alliance and battle against national oppression—remain central to world politics today. $21. Also in Spanish.

## The History of the Russian Revolution
**LEON TROTSKY**

A classic account of the social, economic, and political dynamics of the first socialist revolution as told by one of its central leaders. "The history of a revolution is for us first of all a history of the forcible entrance of the masses into the realm of rulership over their own destiny," Trotsky writes. Unabridged edition, 3 vols. in one. $36. Also in Russian.

## The Revolution Betrayed
### What Is the Soviet Union and Where Is It Going?
**LEON TROTSKY**

In 1917 the working class and peasantry of Russia carried out one of the most profound revolutions in history. Yet within ten years a political counterrevolution by a privileged social layer whose chief spokesperson was Joseph Stalin was being consolidated. This classic study of the Soviet workers state and its degeneration illuminates the roots of the social and political crisis in Russia and other countries that formerly made up the Soviet Union. $20. Also in Spanish.

### Capitalism's World Disorder
*Working-Class Politics at the Millennium*
JACK BARNES

The social devastation and financial panic, the coarsening of politics and politics of resentment, the cop brutality and acts of imperialist aggression accelerating around us—all are the product of lawful forces unleashed by capitalism. But the future the propertied classes have in store for us can be changed by the united struggle and selfless action of workers and farmers conscious of their power to transform the world. $24. Also in Spanish and French.

### The Changing Face of U.S. Politics
*Working-Class Politics and the Trade Unions*
JACK BARNES

A handbook for the new generations coming into the factories, mines, and mills, as they react to the uncertain life, ceaseless turmoil, and brutality of capitalism. It shows how millions of working people, as political resistance grows, will revolutionize themselves, their unions and other organizations, and their conditions of life and work. $24. Also in Spanish, French, and Swedish.

### Teamster Rebellion
FARRELL DOBBS

The 1934 strikes that built the industrial union movement in Minneapolis and helped pave the way for the CIO, recounted by a central leader of that battle. The first in a four-volume series on the class-struggle leadership of the strikes and organizing drives that transformed the Teamsters union in much of the Midwest into a fighting social movement and pointed the road toward independent labor political action. $19. Also in Spanish.

## The Communist Manifesto

KARL MARX AND FREDERICK ENGELS

Founding document of the modern working-class movement, published in 1848. Explains why communism is not a set of preconceived principles but the line of march of the working class toward power, "springing from an existing class struggle, a historical movement going on under our very eyes." $5. Also in Spanish.

## Pathfinder Was Born with the October Revolution

MARY-ALICE WATERS

From the writings of Marx, Engels, Lenin, and Trotsky, to the speeches of Malcolm X, Fidel Castro, and Che Guevara, to the words of James P. Cannon, Farrell Dobbs, and leaders of the communist movement in the U.S. today, Pathfinder books aim to "advance the understanding, confidence, and combativity of working people." $3

## We Are Heirs of the World's Revolutions

*Speeches from the Burkina Faso Revolution 1983–87*

THOMAS SANKARA

In five speeches Thomas Sankara explains how the peasants and workers of Burkina Faso established a popular revolutionary government and began to fight the hunger, illiteracy, and economic backwardness imposed by imperialist domination, and the oppression of women inherited from millennia of class society. In so doing, they have provided an example not only to the workers and small farmers of Africa, but to those of the entire world. $10. Also in Spanish and French.

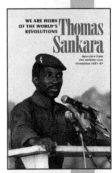

## Cosmetics, Fashions, and the Exploitation of Women

JOSEPH HANSEN, EVELYN REED, MARY-ALICE WATERS

How big business plays on women's second-class status and social insecurities to market cosmetics and rake in profits. The introduction by Mary-Alice Waters explains how the entry of millions of women into the workforce during and after World War II irreversibly changed U.S. society and laid the basis for a renewed rise of struggles for women's emancipation. $15

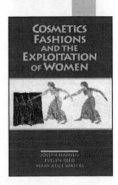

# EXPAND *Your Revolutionary Library*

## Malcolm X Talks to Young People

Four talks and an interview given to young people in Ghana, the United Kingdom, and the United States in the last months of Malcolm's life. This new edition contains the entire December 1964 presentation by Malcolm X at Oxford University in the United Kingdom, in print for the first time anywhere. The collection concludes with two memorial tributes by a young socialist leader to this great revolutionary. $15. Also in Spanish.

## The Working Class and the Transformation of Learning
### *The Fraud of Education Reform under Capitalism*
JACK BARNES

"Until society is reorganized so that education is a human activity from the time we are very young until the time we die, there will be no education worthy of working, creating humanity." $3. Also in Spanish, French, Icelandic, Swedish, and Farsi.

## Socialism: Utopian and Scientific
FREDERICK ENGELS

Modern socialism is not a doctrine, Engels explains, but a working-class movement growing out of the establishment of large-scale capitalist industry and its social consequences. $10

## Revolutionary Continuity
### *Marxist Leadership in the U.S.*
FARRELL DOBBS

How successive generations of fighters took part in struggles of the U.S. labor movement, seeking to build a leadership that could advance the class interests of workers and small farmers and link up with fellow toilers around the world. Two volumes: *The Early Years: 1848–1917*, $20. *Birth of the Communist Movement: 1918–1922*, $19.

**www.pathfinderpress.com**

## Capitalism and the Transformation of Africa

*Reports from Equatorial Guinea*

MARY-ALICE WATERS AND MARTÍN KOPPEL

An account of the transformation of production and class relations in this central African country, as it is drawn deeper into the world market and both a capitalist class and modern proletariat are born. Here also the example of Cuba's socialist revolution comes alive in the collaboration of Cuban volunteer medical brigades helping to transform social conditions. Woven together, the outlines of a future to be fought for today can be seen—a future in which the toilers of Africa have more weight in world politics than ever before. $10. Also in Spanish.

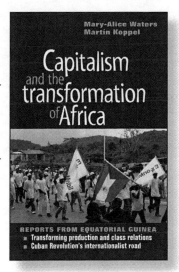

## The Struggle for a Proletarian Party

JAMES P. CANNON

"The workers of America have power enough to topple the structure of capitalism at home and to lift the whole world with them when they rise," Cannon asserts. On the eve of World War II, a founder of the communist movement in the U.S. defends the program and party-building course of the Communist International in Lenin's time. $22

## America's Revolutionary Heritage

*Marxist Essays*

EDITED BY GEORGE NOVACK

A historical materialist analysis of key chapters in the history of the United States, from the genocide against Native Americans to the American Revolution, the Civil War, the rise of industrial capitalism, and the first wave of the fight for women's rights. $25

## The Jewish Question

*A Marxist Interpretation*

ABRAM LEON

Leon traces the historical rationalizations of anti-Semitism to the fact that, in the centuries preceding the domination of industrial capitalism, Jews emerged as a "people-class" of merchants, moneylenders, and traders. He explains why the propertied rulers incite renewed Jew-hatred in the epoch of capitalism's decline. $20

www.pathfinderpress.com

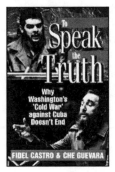

## Playa Girón/Bay of Pigs
*Washington's First Military Defeat in the Americas*

FIDEL CASTRO, JOSÉ RAMÓN FERNÁNDEZ

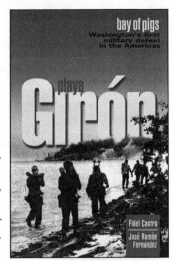

In fewer than 72 hours of combat in April 1961, Cuba's revolutionary armed forces defeated a U.S.-organized invasion by 1,500 mercenaries. In the process, the Cuban people set an example for workers, farmers, and youth the world over that with political consciousness, class solidarity, courage, and revolutionary leadership, one can stand up to enormous might and seemingly insurmountable odds—and win. $20. Also in Spanish.

## Che Guevara Talks to Young People

ERNESTO CHE GUEVARA

In eight talks from 1959 to 1964, the Argentine-born revolutionary challenges youth of Cuba and the world to study, to work, to become disciplined. To join the front lines of struggles, small and large. To politicize their organizations and themselves. To become a different kind of human being as they strive together with working people of all lands to transform the world. $15. Also in Spanish.

## Marianas in Combat
*Teté Puebla and the Mariana Grajales Women's Platoon in Cuba's Revolutionary War 1956–58*

TETÉ PUEBLA

Brig. Gen. Teté Puebla joined the struggle to overthrow the U.S.-backed dictatorship of Fulgencio Batista in 1956, at age 15. This is her story—from clandestine action in the cities, to officer in the Rebel Army's first all-women's unit—the Mariana Grajales Women's Platoon. For 50 years, the fight to transform the social and economic status of women has been inseparable from Cuba's socialist revolution. $14. Also in Spanish.

## Dynamics of the Cuban Revolution
*A Marxist Appreciation*

JOSEPH HANSEN

How did the Cuban Revolution unfold? Why does it represent an "unbearable challenge" to U.S. imperialism? What political obstacles has it overcome? Written as the revolution advanced from its earliest days. $25

# New International

A MAGAZINE OF MARXIST POLITICS AND THEORY

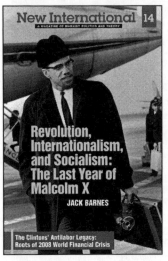

## NEW INTERNATIONAL NO. 14
## Revolution, Internationalism, and Socialism: The Last Year of Malcolm X

*Jack Barnes*

"To understand Malcolm's last year is to see how, in the imperialist epoch, revolutionary leadership of the highest political capacity, courage, and integrity converges with communism. That truth has even greater weight today as billions around the world, in city and countryside, from China to Brazil, are being hurled into the modern class struggle by the violent expansion of world capitalism."—Jack Barnes

*Issue #14 also includes* "The Clintons' Antilabor Legacy: Roots of the 2008 World Financial Crisis"; "The Stewardship of Nature Also Falls to the Working Class: In Defense of Land and Labor" and "Setting the Record Straight on Fascism and World War II." $14

## NEW INTERNATIONAL NO. 12
## Capitalism's long hot winter has begun

*Jack Barnes*

*and "Their Transformation and Ours,"*
*Resolution of the Socialist Workers Party*

Today's sharpening interimperialist conflicts are fueled both by the opening stages of what will be decades of economic, financial, and social convulsions and class battles, and by the most far-reaching shift in Washington's military policy and organization since the U.S. buildup toward World War II. Class-struggle-minded working people must face this historic turning point for imperialism, and draw satisfaction from being "in their face" as we chart a revolutionary course to confront it. $16

ALL THESE ISSUES ARE ALSO AVAILABLE IN SPANISH AND MOST IN FRENCH AT
WWW.PATHFINDERPRESS.COM

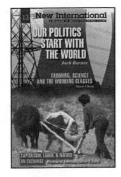

NEW INTERNATIONAL NO. 13
# OUR POLITICS START WITH THE WORLD
*Jack Barnes*

The huge economic and cultural inequalities between imperialist and semicolonial countries, and among classes within almost every country, are produced, reproduced, and accentuated by the workings of capitalism. For vanguard workers to build parties able to lead a successful revolutionary struggle for power in our own countries, says Jack Barnes in the lead article, our activity must be guided by a strategy to close this gap.

*Also includes:* "Farming, Science, and the Working Classes" *by Steve Clark* and "Capitalism, Labor, and Nature: An Exchange" *by Richard Levins, Steve Clark.* $14

NEW INTERNATIONAL NO. 11
# U.S. IMPERIALISM HAS LOST THE COLD WAR
*Jack Barnes*

Contrary to imperialist expectations at the opening of the 1990s in the wake of the collapse of regimes across Eastern Europe and the USSR claiming to be communist, the workers and farmers there have not been crushed. Nor have capitalist social relations been stabilized. The toilers remain an intractable obstacle to imperialism's advance, one the exploiters will have to confront in class battles and war. $16

NEW INTERNATIONAL NO. 8
# CHE GUEVARA, CUBA, AND THE ROAD TO SOCIALISM
*Articles by Ernesto Che Guevara, Carlos Rafael Rodríguez, Carlos Tablada, Mary-Alice Waters, Steve Clark, Jack Barnes*

Exchanges from the opening years of the Cuban Revolution and today on the political perspectives defended by Guevara as he helped lead working people to advance the transformation of economic and social relations in Cuba. $10

NEW INTERNATIONAL NO. 3
# COMMUNISM AND THE FIGHT FOR A POPULAR REVOLUTIONARY GOVERNMENT: 1848 TO TODAY
*Mary-Alice Waters*

Traces the continuity in the fight by the working-class movement over 150 years to wrest political power from the small minority of wealthy property owners, whose class rule, Waters says, is inseparably linked to the "misery, hunger, and disease of the great majority of humanity." *Also includes* "'A Nose for Power': Preparing the Nicaraguan Revolution" *by Tomás Borge.* $13

**PATHFINDER AROUND THE WORLD**

Visit our website for a complete list of titles and to place orders

# www.pathfinderpress.com

PATHFINDER DISTRIBUTORS

### UNITED STATES
*(and Caribbean, Latin America, and East Asia)*

*Pathfinder Books, 306 W. 37th St., 10th Floor,
New York, NY 10018*

### CANADA

*Pathfinder Books, 7105 St. Hubert, Suite 106F,
Montreal, QC H2S 2N1*

### UNITED KINGDOM
*(and Europe, Africa, Middle East, and South Asia)*

*Pathfinder Books, First Floor, 120 Bethnal Green Road
(entrance in Brick Lane), London E2 6DG*

### SWEDEN

*Pathfinder böcker, Bildhuggarvägen 17, S-121 44 Johanneshov*

### AUSTRALIA
*(and Southeast Asia and the Pacific)*

*Pathfinder, Level 1, 3/281-287 Beamish St., Campsie, NSW 2194
Postal address: P.O. Box 164, Campsie, NSW 2194*

### NEW ZEALAND

*Pathfinder, 7 Mason Ave. (upstairs), Otahuhu, Auckland
Postal address: P.O. Box 3025, Auckland 1140*